'Hussain's humour is never complacent; it is the opposite of a defence mechanism (we are encouraged to imagine such a thing) and wryly sidesteps the bad binary of conservative withdrawal as set against algorithm-envenomed hyperassertion. He puts into words a new masculinity maturer than we deserve, that acknowledges swerves of defiance to be inseparable from underswells of doubt.'

– Vidyan Ravinthiran, author of
The Million-Petalled Flower of Being Here

PRAISE FOR *SKY WRI TEI NGS*

'While most of us use airport codes only functionally, Nasser Hussain uses them poetically. Out of the raw material of these unpromising nuggets, he has assembled, ingeniously, an entire book of poems ... It is powerful to see these foundational myths reconstituted out of bureaucratic mundanity – like a model of the human genome built out of Legos.'

– Sam Anderson, *New York Times*

'Hussain's work invites us into a refreshing conceptual lift-off ... Hussain's SKY WRI TEI NGS propel us across literary categories, with turbo-wit, into CON CCP TUA LLY daring altitudes.'

– Margaret Christakos, *Arc Poetry*

'Hussain's surprising leaps remap these banal codes into astonishingly free and funny articulations.'

– Gregory Betts, *Canadian Literature*

first edition

Published with the generous assistance of the Canada Council for the Arts and the Ontario Arts Council. Coach House Books also acknowledges the support of the Government of Canada through the Canada Book Fund.

LIBRARY AND ARCHIVES CANADA CATALOGUING IN PUBLICATION

Title: Love language / poetry by Nasser Hussain.
Names: Hussain, Nasser, author.
Identifiers: Canadiana (print) 20230468411 | Canadiana (ebook) 2023046842X | ISBN 9781552454718 (softcover) | ISBN 9781770567788 (EPUB) | ISBN 9781770567795 (PDF)
Subjects: LCGFT: Poetry.
Classification: LCC PR6108.U77 L68 2023 | DDC 821/.92—dc23

Love Language is available as an ebook: ISBN 978 1 77056 778 8 (EPUB), ISBN 9781770567795 (PDF)

Purchase of the print version of this book entitles you to a free digital copy. To claim your ebook of this title, please email sales@chbooks.com with proof of purchase. (Coach House Books reserves the right to terminate the free digital download offer at any time.)

LOVE LANG UAGE

poetry by

NASSER HUSSAIN

Coach House Books, Toronto

for UNA (who missed the previous flight)

TABLE OF CONTENTS

SING

alove blove clove dlove
 elove flove glove
hlove ilove jlove klove
llovemlovenloveoloveplove
qlove rlove slove
tlove ulove vlove
wlove xlove
ylove
&love
zlove

LOVE POEM

I love Susan's poem 'without you'

I love Charles's poem 'My/My/My'

I love Barrie's poem 'blues'

I love Simina's poem 'cloudburst'

I love William's poem 'Sonnet LV'

I love Walt's poem 'Song of Myself'

I love Zaffar's poem 'Prayer'

I love Vidyan's poem 'The Lecture'

I love Nicole's poem 'succular'

I love Kayo's poem 'Guide to Proper Mixtape Assembly'

I love Kaveh's poem 'Orchids Are Sprouting from the Floorboards'

I love Ken's poem 'Day 1: Apollo Spacecraft'

I love Ron's poem 'Ketjak'

I love Ian's poem 'It Is Possible to Move On Without Moving
    Forward'

I love Adam's poem 'Try to Praise the Mutilated World'

I love Matthew's poem 'Squid Squad, #1–64'

I love Jane's poem 'On Ninjas'

I love Moez's poem 'Day'

I love Jordan's poem *what is in the stomach is carried in the head*

I love Claudia's untitled sequence of texts in second person
    called 'I'

I love n.h.'s poem 'Love'

I love Lila's poem 'Peaches'

I love Vladimir's poem 'The Poet Worker'

I love Christian's poem *Eunoia*

I love Derek's poem 'Prose of the Trans-Canada'

I love Wayne's poem 'one story goes a man on his lunch break
    was hit'

I love Harry's poem 'Quality Aspects of Carrots'

I love Rishi's poem '#MyEngland'

I love J. R.'s poem 'Once Upon a Tide'

I love Anthony/Vahni's poem 'Two Foreign'

I love Fred's poem 'Bullet'

I love Gary's poem 'The Birth of Writing'

I love Laila's poem 'all your grandmothers have stopped cooking'

I love Jordan's poem *'mouth implies room; room mimics mouth.'*

I love Donato's poem 'ligature'

I love James's poem 'para-mental'

I love Keshia's poem 'Window-Smashing'

I love William's poem 'Portrait of a Lady'

I love Arji's poem 'Don't take this the wrong way but'

I love Jonah's poem 'Based on Actual Events / Attempts to
    Survive the Apocalypse'

I love Sandeep's poem 'No Title'

IF I HAD TO SAY

I'd say
it started
way back
when a
cave person
made a
grunt speak
the name
of the
thing that
they made
& maybe
the brain
of the
cave person's
mate caved
in at
the way
the grunt
said so
much with
such sight
so in
the light
of their
own light
& in
the shade

of their
own cave
they sang
about what
a great
game they
had made
& they
brayed – let's
play it
again &
again &
again – make
some rules
& betray
them – make
some tools
& then
break them
until every
thing knows
that its
name is
made of
us.

READING

(look!)

DISCORDANT JOT

for Jordan Scott

say this sentence once. do this four times.
what's a ghazal, again? just an old person's intuition.

blur these entence once. dude, form ore dimes?
The Age of Huts deserves to win. language as pattern recognition.

blurp his intensenesses. derp de derp or hi-de-highs.
insert sentence here, & there. land gauge, arranged grange –
    a garden.

blurt 'the entrants won!' yup, you sure did, sire.
nsrt sntnc hr, nd thr. I'm the rules, but you're the maker.

PERFORMANCE REPORT

you are a proven asset to the team; you have shown up on
    time, you are considerate & kind, you have a great
    rapport with the kids, &

Thad said he likes how you clean your keyboard, but
    that said, you're slow with your reports & the parents
    have some queries, &

Chad said that Thad said your hair is a mystery, but
    that said, the coffee station is immaculate
    so thanks for that, but

Fred said that Chad said that Thad said that not everyone
    is hired on 'merit' winkwink &
    that said, some of us would appreciate
    it if you stopped blowing kisses, but

the head of HR said that Thad needs to get
    his head checked, &
    that said, no one disputes the quality
    of your out-of-office replies, but

when you see Thad don't mention
    what's being said
    about what he said, &

that said, we'd like it if you were out
    of the office next Weds but
    after Thad's been read
    the riot act we can talk
    about next steps, &

that said, you've been a thoroughbred, but
that said, we think you're an ass, but
that said

                        see you Monday

THINKING OF YOU

think of time as a lemon
& the pith as naps

think of time as a pen
& the ink as space

think of time as a cat
& the claw as reminder

think of time as stone
& your hand that holds it

think of time as a teacher
& poems are homework

think of time as a lantern
& who has a lantern

think of time as a wallet
& money's no object

think of time as a myth
& the teller is geology

think of time as a lover
& physics is a kiss

WHAT HAPPENED TO YOU, LOVE

I don't feel like we talk anymore

I've been calling tried you on whatsapp double blue checkmark
but you didn't get back to me

(three … s)

I say your name to everyone I meet
I'm lowkey stalking you
I'm learning about tone tags: /lh /P /pos
yo, so: even if the lights go out even if my thumb grows numb
even if my bottom falls out even if my roof leaks even if the
battery dies even if the coffee cools even if the verdict's wrong
even if the vote's recalled even if the absurd is just surd even if
sand falls through the hourglass even if we get distracted by
the fact that sand falling in an hourglass made out of sand itself
might just be the best metaphor for time we could ask for –
we're passing thru different states of ourselves – even if we run
out of milk, words, ink, bread, ozone, & bees even if we beat
the odds & break even even if the day is rough & unfair even if
my teeth break even if my voice cracks if my back spasms or
my heart attacks or my brain strokes even if the only way to
swallow my tongue is to put my foot in my mouth & eat my
own boot

I want to talk with you

SOCIAL CONTRACT(ION)

stuff is made for
a fee

but is everywhere in
supply chains

I WANT TO LOVE EVERYTHING, BUT

I am
not my
old dog

(he knew
which words
to chew)

TL;DR, OR, MOLLY GOT AN IPHONE

for db

do you agree to these
terms and conditions[1]

[1]yes dear terms and conditions yes too numerous to mention yes I'll hand over all my yes personal information yes I'll let you track my location yes in case of water damage I won't sue yes I'm ready to input my whole life into you yes I agree yes keep me updated yes I won't meddle with the hardware no I don't need to pay more for the guarantee of care because I'm betting you'll outlast the warranty yes I'm over eighteen yes here's my password yes in fact I have nothing to hide yes I hate the time it takes to sync yes remind me but I probably won't bother yes it's automatic but sexily so [yes] yes you're more form than function which makes you supremely functional yes I can't function without you yes I'm a third G in a world of fives yes I said I agree yes quit pestering me yes I'll do it tomorrow (yes I won't) yes I agree I agree I agree yes yes yes yes yes yes yes yes yes yes yesyesyes yesyesyesyesyesyesyesyesyesyesyesyesyesyes yesyesyesyesyesyesyesyesyesyesyesyesyesyes yesyesyesyesyesyesyesyesyesyesyesyesyesyes yesyesyesyesyesyesyesyesyesyesyesyesyesyes yesyesyesyesyesyesyesyesyesyesyesyesyesyes yesyesyesyesyesyesyesyesyesyesyesyesyesyes yesyesyesyesyesyesyesyesyesyesyesyesyesyes yesyesyesyesyesyesyesyesyesyesyesyesyesyes yesyesyesyesyesyesyesyesyesyesyesyesyesyes yesyesyesyesyesyesyesyesyesyesyesyesyesyes yesyesyesyesyesyesyesyesyesyesyesyesyesyes yesyesyesyesyesyesyesyesyesyesyesyesyesyes yesyesyesyesyesyesyesyesyesyesyesyesyesyes yesyesyesyesyesyesyesyesyesyesyesyesyesyes yesyesyesyesyesyesyesyesyesyesyesyesyesyes
I do

YOU'RE THE FIRST LAW

love isn't chemistry   it's physics

I know because I was broken apart by pure force, my mass
shattered by the inertia of twenty-six dumb years, but some
molecule of me got caught in the clinamen & was multiplied
by the acceleration of you who glanced & swerved & looped
back to me, & you, in spite of all probability, moved into the
same place at the same time (who would've theorized it) &
fused me into a new element which is true

even if it's unobservable ut
terly uncertain & unrepeatable

(which is great)

because that
is precisely the moment

when science   transmutes   into art

& for one fundamentally random aggregate
of atoms that everyone calls nasser
the firmament had begun to hum
at a frequency so familiar

I called it   home

YOUR LANGUAGE IS all curve & slow & form & worn & wound & smooth & squeeze & breathe & wool & warmth & true & yes & /pos & post & hi & design & bells & whistles & schooling & books & soft & spines & meat & sweat & funk & prince & hands & splayed & rain & gluten & music & grand & generous & magnanimous & unanimous & random & rhythm & rhyme & pattern & banter & words & wonder & words & joy & words & words & words & words

I WANT TO LOVE EVERYTHING, BUT

I am
not my
old dog

(he knew
which words
to chew)

I REALLY WANT TO LOVE EVERYTHING, BUT

it's tough
with all
these alerts

my phone
burps &
I suppress

the urge
to change
that word

I REALLY REALLY WANT TO LOVE EVERYTHING, BUT

some folx
are actively

producing fake
houseplants instead

of watering
real ones

what buds?
I'm confused

I REALLY REALLY *REALLY* WANT TO LOVE EVERYTHING, BUT

there's folx
who don't

believe reason
& folx

who won't
revise canons

& folx
who'll say

the word
folx sux

& I
think shux –

how the
fux do

I spell
real change

APOCALYPSE SONG

for Basil Chiasson

oh the battery	it's running low
oh the amazon	she's getting slow
oh the weather	don't listen no more
oh the flowchart	ain't got that flow
I'll find the shovel	& you grab the fretboard
I'll make the baked beans	& you guard the seed hoard
I'll be the message	& you be the medium
I'll make the faces	& you keep on feedin' 'em
but wooo-hooo's	got the mon-ey?
wooo-hoo's	got the memo?
wooooo-hooo's	got the mon-ey, the money, the money?
oh the wavelength	it's getting flat
no oscillations	are coming back
I think we might be	all on our lonesome
leave the drone there	we gotta go, son
you fix the wires	& I'll flick the switches
you break the bottle	& I'll catch the liquid
the rain ain't falling	it's just more insistent
there might be	a preview after the credits

but woo-hooo's   got the password?
woo-hooo's   got the privilege?

oh who
woo-hoo
woo-hooooooo's   got the money?

EXPLICIT/ELICIT

feel sad
now feel bad
now feel jealous
now feel overzealous
now feel just zealous enough
now feel sad, but a different sad from the first sad
now feel sad badly
now feel bad sadly
now peel back a layer
now peel an onion
now feel cute, might delete later
now don't feel sad anymore
now cry a little
now feel uncomfortable
now feel literal
now feel feral
now feel literate
now feel obdurate
now feel obstinate
now feel abdominal stretch
now feel apocalyptic
now feel apoplectic
pow! feel impacted
now feel fully present
now feel like it's never ending
now feel like it's ending
now feel like its ending

POEM WITH DELIBERATE BLANKS IN IT

I say something. & you say something in italics. there is. you
could be a this & a that at the same time. the thing over there is
some stuff. it might pulsate or throb. there is air in the space
that is reminding. a thought locks on to an object. the object
starts to behave a bit differently. I decide that it's in love. real
things with tangible surfaces reassert themselves into the space
between sentences   .   a claim is made about realism.
the absence of personal characteristics is *coded* but neither of
us is going to admit anything. I'm inviting you but not inviting
you to share this intimacy that is not intimate. I've shared this
private thing, now. you say another thing. it intersects an object
in the room, which is a real room, but not the room you're in
now, so is it a real room at all anymore. there's a memory.

EMBODY, BUDDY

the tooth of my body
the nail of my body
the hair of my body
the skin of my body
the pupil of my body
the finger of my body
the ink of my body
the spine of my body
the appendix of my body
the print of my body
the back of my body
the circuit of my body
the mouth of my body
the chamber of my body
the anvil of my body
the beat of my body
the popliteal space of my body
the phiz of my body
the bridle of my body
the apple of my body
the valves of my body
the crypts of my body
the hole of my body
the roof of my body
the duct of my body
the bone of my body
the bottom of my body
the little grape of my body

the circle of willis of my body
the pneumonoultramicroscopicsilicovolcanoconiosis of my body
the air of my body
the water of my body
the thrapple of my body
the tongue of my body
the lace of my body
the eye of my body
the sole of my body
the ridge of my body
the sartorius of my body
the scar of my body
the pinna of my body
the pit of my body
the gut of my body
the skull of my body
the mind of my body
the lump of my body
the palm of my body
the islets of my body
the delta of my body
the stone of my body
the mineral of my body
the gas of my body
the electricity of my body
the cup of my body
the pump of my body
the enamel of my body
the window of my body
the bed of my body

the snuff box of my body
the ring of my body
the shingles of my body
the nerve of my body
the gall of my body
the cheek of my body
the drum of my body
the drum of my body
the drum of my body
the heel of my body

the bodies of my body

(I FIXED IT FOR YOU)

E=N=G=L=I=S=H

THERE WAS THIS MAYAKOVSKY POEM ABOUT QUITTING SMOKING & I'M PRETTY SURE it was autobiographical & in it the speaker had just quit smoking like for a day & was jumping & leaping about in a world refreshed & full of beauty & smells & colour & energy & everyone was sexier & food tasted better & their clothes felt more comfortable & the water was clearer & their breath was better & they mention the food a few more times & everything is written in short punchy lines & lots & lots of exclamation points & the poem runs all over three pages in a breathless romp that clearly mirrors the speaker's truth & the speaker's truth is really close to the poet's truth but that's the thing about a good poem you can't quite say to your audience that it's you who's speaking because poems are supposed to be like slogans in that they just appear out of nowhere & solve some complicated problem you have with nothing more than a few words arranged in a pleasing way but back to Mayakovsky & how the voice in the poem both is & isn't his & I wonder if he ever quit smoking for good because when you do it's better than any poem but Maya-kovsky's is a really excellent try & the point I wanted to make is that the way Mayakovsky or Mayakovsky's speaker feels about quitting smoking is how I feel when I think of you IRL but there's no way I can say it in a poem even though it is

true

SAY WHAT YOU WILL, BUT

you can't say seagulls without eagles
you can't say welcome without whelk
you can't say god without odd
you can't say syllable without ill & a bull
you can't say harmony without money
you can't say say without a
you can't say paper without kinda whispering her
you can't say humpback whale without smiling
but you *can* say happiness without a penis
you can't say coffee without cough
you can't say reading without more reading
you can't say volume without you
you can't say comparison without Paris
you can't say porcelain without poor Celan
you can't say blackberries without Ponge
you can't say backpack without ack ack
you can't say backache without cake
you can't say sciatica without attic
you can't say hurt without her
you can't say yurt without yer
you can't say blurt without blur
you can't say curt without cur
you can't say words without whirr

THIS IS *YOUR* LANGUAGE, I'M JUST SPEAKING IT

Inglish folx keep it to themselves
Engloss folx forget what they got
an Englush lunch is three pints of bitter
Englisp is a slip of the lung
Englishhh, my babe – go to bed
in pain, say Anguish
Canadians get pert near the truth (Englishish)
don't proffread, just Languish
get its autograph: Fanglish

detourne it: Unglish

Thinglish is the dialect of nouns & Winglish is the shisper of
    butterflies & ornithologists in Point Pelee
you're singleish on Tinder, but don't DM your former lover –
    that's Exlish
blow it up, watch it Banglish
when it's over it's Endglish
ouch you darn bee –> Stinglish

or slide with it & just glish, glish, glish

eeeng

anglish
english
inglish
onglish
unglish

eeenglish
ennnglish
enggglish
englllish
engliiish
englisssh
englishhh

english
eenngglliisshh
eeennngggglllliiissshhh
eeeennnnngggggllllliiiiissssshhhhh
eeeeeennnnnggggggllllllliiiiiissssssshhhhhh
eeeeeeennnnnngggggggllllllliiiiiiisssssssshhhhhhh
eeeeeeeennnnnnnnggggggggglllllllliiiiiiiiissssssssssshhhhhhhhh
eeeeeeeennnnnnnngggggggggllllllllliiiiiiiiisssssssssshhhhhhhhh
eeeeeeennnnnnnggggggggllllllliiiiiiiisssssssshhhhhhhh
eeeeeennnnnnggggggglllllliiiiiissssssshhhhhh
eeeeennnnngggggllllliiiiissssshhhhh
eeeennnngggglllliiiisssshhhh
eeennnggggllliiissshhh
eennggglliisshh
english

lishh

ENGLISH LIT. english litany. english lite. english literacy. english literal. english literalism. english literalist. english literalistic. english literality. english literalize. english literally. english literariness. english literary. english literate. english literati. english literatim. english literation. english literato. english literator. english literatus. english liters. english lites. english lith. english lithe. english lithemia. english litheness. english lither. english lithesome. english lithia. english lithiasis. english lithic. english lithium. english lithographer. english lithography. english lithosphere. english Lithuanian. english litigant. english litigate. english litigation. english litigious. english litigiousness. english litigiousness-ness. english litigiousness-ness-esque. english litigosity. english litmus. english litotes. english litre. english litter. english litterateur. english litterbug. english litterer. english little. english little bitty. english little by little. english little finger. english littling. english littoral. english lituate. english lit up. english liturgical. english liturgiological. english liturgy. english litz.

THAT POETIC EXERCISE IN WHICH THE PIECE IS COMPOSED ENTIRELY OF QUESTIONS, THIS TIME BY A PERSON OF COLOUR

is it me? is it just me? is it possible that you didn't see me? what does visible mean? what did you just say? did I hear that correctly? is she looking at me? are you kidding me? isn't this enough? what are you doing? will you let go of me? can't you tell? what's your problem, buddy? is that inclusive? have you ever had a person of colour be your teacher? how many? can I kick it? does that include breakfast? why doesn't that person have to? why would you think it was me? why wouldn't you think it was me? where are *you from, no really?* did you not see me right there? can you not hear what I'm saying? am I the only one who saw that? are you kidding me? you want how much? why would I be carrying ID? how did they get in? is it just me? am I missing something? can you feel it? can you feel it? can you feel it? can I ask what the problem is? can I get a look at that file? is there a problem here? are you okay? can I get a drink? can I get a glass of water here? can you speak? can you walk? are you able to breathe? are you alone out here? are you lost? can I help you? can I get anything for you, sir? how can I be of assistance? can I get a witness? how's the wife and kids? how's the golf swing coming along? Hey, Thad, how about that weather, eh? how do you pronounce that? Fockner? Phalk-nürr? where do you want me? is this above or below my pay grade? do I look like I work here? would you mind? would you just look out? would you please get out of the way? would you mind? would you just look at this? would you live like this? would you take this shit? would you say that to my face? would

(45)

you agree that the author is properly dead now? can you grab that? would you just shut up? what's the problem here? what's the issue, man? what's the overriding concern, pal? what's the password again? what's the code? where's the switch? what's the word for that? what's the way to sit? what's the width of a line? can I kick it? what are they thinking? am I being tedious? am I repeating myself? is anyone listening? did they not just hear me say that? is this what paranoia feels like? this isn't just an exercise, is it? would you like me to continue?

SIMPLE MATH

birth of sucker to minute ratio = 1:1

one peck of dirt/diet

set of birds in hand = $[2 \times (\text{birds in bushes})]$

grass's hue of greenness when underfoot < hue of greenness
    on other side

ratio of measurements to cuts = 2:1

1st cut = maximum depth

infinity = opportunities taken to hurt the one you love

late > never

love = $0 \times$ sorries articulated

complete set of first-person singulars in team = $[0]$

density of blood > H_2O

$$\frac{\text{flies}}{\text{honey}} > \frac{\text{flies}}{\text{vinegar}}$$

daily intake = 1 × fish whereas lifetime intake = learning to angle

give > receive

sword < pen

nod = wink

change = rest

1 stitch now = 9 later

volume of actions > volume of words

1¢ = exchange value of your thoughts

weak link = chain

location of hook for hat = home = location of heart

desirable number of eggs per basket = $(n - 1)$, where n
represents the complete set of eggs in your possession

NO REALLY IT'S HONESTLY NOTHING

a zero isn't
a number it's
a drawing

a drawing isn't
a nything more than
a drawing

a drawing is
a zero trying to look like
a something

**DOES ANYONE REALLY KNOW HOW TO USE
THAT RESEALABLE TAB ON A BAG OF RICE &
IF THEY DO CAN THEY PLEASE GET IN TOUCH
WITH ME @NASSERSHUSSAIN BECAUSE I AM
WATCHING TOO MANY TEN-MINUTE SELF-
IMPROVEMENT VIDEOS**

because I'm starting to think that
everything is do-it-yourself-able

all the tools you need are to hand – behold as
flat surfaces curve in the gravitational field
of my broadband-borrowed acumen

I have no father, but I got algorithm

– hey presto, my desko
transforms into a sous-vide
steak perfectly medium rare & yes
terday I took inches off my inseam
with a belt sander & an eye for retail

there are gaps in my browser history   & basmati all
                                               over the
                                               floor

I'm really
just asking
for a friend

SERIOUSLY UNLIKELY ANIMAL FRIENDSHIPS

jellyfish & marmoset
tiger prawn & snow leopard
wolverines & whistling wolves
paramecium & a pair o' mooses: see 'em?

a festival of rambunctious bumps
       honkers on schnozzes
       peepers to poopers
       gun shows & flexed pipes

manes maul
maws mewl

IF YOU FIND THE BUDDHA IN YOUR phone, add him. if you find the buddha in your spam folder, delete him. if you find the buddha in your bookcase, cull him. if you find the buddha in the fridge, consider eating him, but decide against cooking tonight & order some delivery. if the buddha delivers your order, tip him. if you find the buddha annoying, you're doing it wrong. if you find the buddha in the peloton, draft him. if you find the buddha in the sauna, rhyme him. if you find the buddha in the trash, treasure him. if you find the buddha on the internet, accept all cookies. if you find the buddha in a snowstorm, make a snowman. if you find the buddha in a pickle, make a sandwich. if you find the buddha in a dream, wake him. if you find the buddha in a dictionary, derange him. if you find the buddha in america, you should probably warn him. if you find the buddha in a state of undress, address him. if you find the buddha at my place, call me.

WHAT I WANTED TO SAY IN THAT INTERVIEW IS THAT 'WHAT I WOULD BRING TO THIS INSTITUTION' IS MY EXTENSIVE COLLECTION OF FANCY FOUNTAIN PENS

look, look, look,

> this one has
> violet ink I
> ground the nib

> myself I scraped
> it across a
> whet stone made

> for swords but
> the result was
> satisfying there's variation

> in the line
> it squeaks across
> the itchy page

> my classes will
> be night classes
> I will teach

> exclusively by candlelight
> I'll bring these
> pens & make

every one illuminate

& until the
bell tolls they
will draw their
names & the
names of their
lovers & the
names of their
buddies & the
names of their
hamsters & the
names of their
languages & the
names of their
conditions & the
names of their
names of their
names of their
names & all
the while I'll
hover in the
glow of the
smart board murmuring

                    look, look, look,

I'M IN a rut. I'm in a funk. I'm in a slump. I'm in a stump. I'm in a stew pot. I'm in a fetal position. I'm in an office. I'm in an office chair in an office. I'm in the position of being in an office chair, which would seem to imply I'm in an office. I'm in a Muskoka chair but I'm not in Muskoka. I'm in a fugue state. I'm in a state of denial. I'm in love. I'm in a stately home. I'm in Dunrobin Castle, where they have archived all the vacuum cleaners they've ever bought & display them in a row that you walk past when you leave, in a kind of evolutionary pattern, so you can see that technology has changed but people really have not. I'm in a quandary: is any room you work in an office? I'm *on* planet Earth, even when I'm *in* a cave. I'm in tune. I'm in debt. I'm in a state of perpetual wonder. I'm in choate. I'm in a decisive mood. I'm in decisive. I'm in England. I'm in Yorkshire. I'm in Leeds. I'm in the city centre. I'm in the way. I'm in discreet. I'm in violation. I'm in violets. I'm in a viola. I'm in a gaddadavida. I'm into you. I'm in your DMs. I'm into all that. I'm in ternet. I'm in lust. I'm in a meeting soon. I'm in tongues. I'm in Quixote. I'm in your head. I'm inchoate. I'm inbetween-states. I'm in peril. I'm in distress. I'm in a dress. I'm at this address. I'm in doors. I'm in a jar. I'm in explicable. I'm in teresting. I'm still in school. I'm in terred, well not just yet. I'm in a Muskoka state of mind. I'm in earnest. I'm in an urn. I'm in a vacuum cleaner bag. I'm in a nest. I'm in a digital ideological bubble blown out of my own hot air. I'm in charge. I'm in language. No, you are.

vibe(((
((
((
((
((
((
((
((
((
((
((
((
((
((
((
(((((((((((((((((((((((((((.))))))))))))))))))))))))
))
))
))
))
))
))
))
))
))
))
))
))
))
))rate

FOR EVERYBODY ON YOUR WEDDING DAY

Michelle loves the way Betsy talks & Betsy loves the way Charlotte smokes & Charlotte loves the way London moves & London doesn't really care about us but Charlotte loves the way Zeynep smiles & Zeynep loves the way Matt sands & Matt loves the way Sam screams & Sam loves the way Eric pours whisky & Eric loves the way Rob writes & Rob loves the way Colin arrives & Colin loves the way Dom argues & Dom loves the way Annette collects & Annette loves the way Kaley gets excited & Kaley loves the way Jeff makes fake maple syrup for his English friends but keeps the good stuff for his Canadian ones & Jeff loves the way Daniel sings & Daniel loves the way Anna teaches & Anna loves the way Anna dresses & Anna loves the way Dom argues & Dom loves the way Ben tilts & Ben loves the way Caroline is so smart & Caroline loves the way Susan is so considerate & Susan loves the way Gillian knits & Gillian loves the way Edel studies Icelandic sagas & Edel loves the way Betsy smokes & Betsy loves the way Yeliz talks & Yeliz loves the way Milena watches *Friends* & Milena loves the way Dom argues & Dom loves the way Gareth plays & Gareth loves the way Catherine plays & Catherine loves the way James plays & James loves the way Dom argues & Dom loves the way Milena loves Dom & Milena loves the way Dom loves Milena & I love the way

& WHEN LIFE GIVES

you melons make melodies
      & when life gives
you samples make simplicities
      & when life gives
you salmons make similarities
      & when life gives
you marbles make da vincis
      & when life gives
you warnings make cigarillos
      & when life gives
you up make makeup sex
      & when life gives
you love make alphabets
      & when life gives
you umpires make sport of it
      & when life gives
you signs make signatories
      & when life gives
you songs make up a story
      & when life gives
you possums make possibilities
      & when life gives
you television make documentaries
      & when life gives
you language make ~~mixtapes~~ mistakes

A POEM FOR ADAM ZAGAJEWSKI IN EARLY 2021

this book of yours that arrived today
tells me you were born in 1945

(which makes you old enough to be my father)
(which is true (because I think my father was born

around 1945) (I say 'I think' because I don't
know for sure & you can take that for what it means) but

in any case I think I would have liked you) (I already like
you) (by which I mean we would have gotten

along) I like the way your line breaks (your mind
works) the way you (probably) held a glass

of milk ((or wine) (or whisky) (they're all the same you'd
    claim)) & quaff (does anyone quaff anything these days)

that seems like an anachronism (even for a poet)
& it doesn't even bother me when you think
about poems (even as you write them)

(every new year's eve my father would make choux pastry &
pipe it into rows of S shapes & buns that he'd bake so slowly
they would remain as pale as possible & he'd split the buns in
two & stick the S & the halves of the bun into a ball of whipped
cream & spoon the ball with the pastry stuck into it onto a

saucer filled with sieved raspberry coulis & when the waiters walked to your table with the saucer held up high & swooped down to serve you the dessert it was revealed that the flamboyancy of the waiter's gait from the kitchen to the table would nudge the cream across the plate so that a white swirl would slice through the red liquid & the people would gasp because it looked very much like a little swan swimming across a red pond & maybe that's when I thought about being an artist but dad left before he could show me how to make the swan trick work) (so I started reading instead)

(like my friend Dominic said)

genius is all about
how much
you can forgive

(I'm so
         rry)
it took me

(so) long

WRITE A BOOK MADE OF LAUGHTER & STRAY EYELASHES

write a book made of lost remote controls

write a book made of butt implants

write a book made of carrot tops & ivory soap

write a book made of actual fiction

write a book made of lasers

write a book made of high-fructose corn syrup

write a book made of sales pitches

write a book made of pitch

write a book made of dog ears

write a book made of leaves of grass

write a book made of post-it notes

write a book made of wrought iron

write a book made of amoebas holding hands

write a book made of stubble

write a book made of the ashes of the books you burnt

write a book made of harming the environment

write a book made of carbon neutrality

write a book made of solar panels

write a book made of the supreme court

write a book made of bullets

write a book made of buddies

write a book made of purpose

write a book made of a book made of a book made of a book

[SOUND] + {SOUND} = (IDEA)!

Shush mushes! Loose gooses! Miss mooses! Stash cash! Upend cupid! Group poop! Scratch rashes! Split lips! Fling linguists! Finger lingerings! Worsen gherkins! Fur cups! Screw true! Firm bums! Squirt terms! Squeal deals! Verb herbs! Alarm barns! Charge stars! Blurt words! Burp stirrups! Pop tops off! Cop slots! Laugh gas! Shake aches! Take lakes! Make haste! Pray late! Barricade barracudas! Paper plates! Pure words! Swirl worlds! Stir curds! Alert hermits! Chirp harps! Start art! Heap sheets! Find minds! Eat treats! Write kites! Write lights! Write quite! Fight knights! Injure ninjas! Erotic karate! Dunk dukes! Punch drunks! Flaunt want! Chant grants! Age rings! Rings age! Play lays! Hear ears! Cure ferns! Purge clergy! Feed readers! Teach each! Sneak bleach! Repeat repeat! Work space! Tease fleas! Please lease! Time mimes! Silence licences! Grind tines! Blame stains! Strange days! Stay game! Hate drains! Pair tears! Watch hawks! Talk lots! Know loads! Row boats! Tow floats! Arraign parades! Claim fame! Gay days! Pay grades! Train rain! Heave leaves! Smoke yolks! Align signs! Sing wings! Change things! Things change!

DO WHAT YOU WANT, BUT

for Nick Cox

you can't stumble without tumble
grumble without rumble
strain without rain
mistake without take

you can't shit without hit
thrash without rash
blast without last

you can't burn without urn
strangle without wrangle
appear without peer
appease without peace

(you be the forest, & I'll be the trees
you be the buzz, & I'll be the bees)

& if we think without ink for a sec
I'll bet you a full crock of honey
that we'll see that
things
ing –
which is to say   they verb their
assurances in the susurrance
below the surface of wordness

& you gotta be hollow
to follow all the echoes

or

said differently –

a teacup cups best
when it's empty

so, read & be ready –

cry 'avec'

& let slip
the curs of occurrence

THIS DIS ORIENTATION

for Ian Williams

I get up in the [racialized] morning, put on some [racialized] music. eat a [racialized] breakfast, go for a [racialized] hot yoga session. with [racialized] soap, take a [racialized] shower. read the [racialized] paper. the [racialized] orange juice is sour after [racialized] toothpaste. the [racialized] train is late. the [racialized] conductor makes a hilarious [racialized] announcement. the [racialized] coffee cautions me that its [racialized] contents are hot. I put the [racialized] cup in the [racialized] receptacle. the [racialized] pavement is cracked. I dodge the [racialized] rush-hour foot traffic. swipe my [racialized] staff card at the [racialized] door to my [racialized] office. begin my [racialized] pre-work rituals. look at the [racialized] clock. do a [racialized] mental calculation. [racialized]. [racialized]. in the [racialized] team meeting, we discuss the fact that racialized people do less well in our [racialized] organization. I feel [racialized] rage at the [racialized] fact that no one admits it's simply [racialized] bias. have another [racialized] coffee, even though it might raise my [racialized] blood pressure. mentally check out of [racialized] work. [racialized]. [racialized]. [racialized]. idly scroll a [racialized] social-media website. consider going for a [racialized] beer instead of a [racialized] meal for my [racialized] lunch.

INTERMINGLINGSingingsigningslidingslowingsparingsting
ingstipplingstoppingstartingstarlingswearingswingingslinging
spinningschoolingsippingstaringsprintingswitchingsticking
shiftingstrippingslippingswattingslickingsnatchingsplashing
strappingslinkingsinkingsweatingspreadingsurgingspilling
swervingservingslurringstewingstoolingsunningstunningswell
ingsailingsellingstallingsparringsparingsinningswingingstash
ingslashingspanningslappingscapingseeingsteeringstowingslow
ingspooningslurpingsoppingstrongingstrenghteningstretching
sleepingsharingsayingspeakingshirkingsearchings

SWERVEY

we asked 100 firefighters: what do you do when
                    someone says 'intractable'
we asked 100 students: what will you do with
                    this wild & precious life of yours
we asked 100 coffee growers: what's the best part
                    of waking up
we asked 100 game show hosts: where do lost socks go
we asked 100 chefs: name your favourite adjectives
we asked 100 light bulbs: how many people does it take
                    to change you
we asked 100 IT support workers: off or on
we asked 100 FTSE 100 companies: what's for lunch
we asked 100 questions: what's the strangest place
                    you've ever made whoopee
we asked 100 mariners: how long before you can be
                    considered ancient
we asked 100 americans: find a map
we asked 100 adjectives: name your favourite meal
we asked 100 numbers: what's the best letter
we asked 100 books: how is the author, anyway
we asked 100 lawyers: rank your favourite suits
we asked 100 americans: map yourself
we asked 100 emperors: which piece of clothing
                    should you remove first
we asked 100 billionaires: guess the price of a pint of milk
we asked 100 horses: describe the scent of glue
we asked 100 psychics: predict the next question
we asked 100 protesters: which street to take

we asked 100 computers: what wakes you
in the middle of the night

RREEDDLLIINNEE

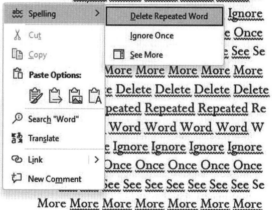

Delete Delete Delete Delete Delete Delete
Repeated Repeated Repeated Repeated Re
Word Word Word Word Word Word W
Ignore Ignore Ignore Ignore Ignore Ignore
Once Once Once Once Once Once Once
See See See See See See See See See See Se
More More More More More More More
Delete Delete Delete Delete Delete Delete
Repeated Repeated Repeated Repeated Re
Word Word Word Word Word Word W

abc Spelling	>	Delete Repeated Word	Ignore
X Cut		Ignore Once	e Once
Copy		See More	See Se
Paste Options:		More More More More More	
		e Delete Delete Delete Delete	
		peated Repeated Repeated Re	
Search "Word"		Word Word Word Word W	
Translate		e Ignore Ignore Ignore Ignore	
Link	>	Once Once Once Once Once	
New Comment		See See See See See See See Se	

More More More More More More More

FROM LANGUAGE, TO LANGUAGE

      language to the left of me, language to the right:
here I am, stuck in the language with you
      of the language, for the language, by the
language
      when they language low, we language high
      a language is haunting Europe
      ashes to languages, language to dust
      the phantom of the language is here
      language come, language go
      language and language went up the language to
fetch a pail of language
      we the language
      here a language, there a language, everywhere
a language language
      a language by any other language would smell
as language
      a language is a language is a language
      when language calls
      ich bin ein Languager
      language on a hot tin language
      for a long language I used to go to language
early
      you language what you language
      language the whirlanguage
      stately, plump Language Mulligan came from
the languagehead, bearing a language of lather on
which a language and a language lay crossed

languaging and languaging in the languaging
gyre / the language cannot hear the languager
there is no language outside the language
it was the language of times, it was the
language of times
it is a language universally languaged that a
single language in possession of a good language must
be in want of a language
o language, my language

O HI

o yah, i'm
fine: just out
here, trying
to believe in
            language
                    like you do

this book is about the rain. this book is about being rejected. this book asks the question: how to write about joy when it isn't safe for everyone, everywhere, always? this book imagines that words don't matter. this book is about how matter matters. this book matters. this book is about figuring out how being humble is a privilege. this book is about figuring out what to destroy, & what to keep, & what to do when two revolutionaries meet for coffee. this book is about a spiderweb in an attic in the arctic. this book is about all the different uses of laughter. this book is about microchips & potato crisps. this book is about what to do when Muhammad Ali is repeatedly asking you rhetorical questions while repeatedly punching you in the face. this book is all the mistakes I've made in public. this book is about the aftershocks of shame. this book is about my dead brother, & how this book can't be about that at all. this book is about using humour as a defence mechanism. this book defers. this book deflects. this book is about how to attend a staff meeting with people who have been microaggressive with you. this book is about how to attend a staff meeting with someone you've been microaggressive toward. this book evades. this book takes the bull by the thorns. this book collects dust, but does so actively, deliberately, turning each mote in its hand, inspecting for flaws & splendours, & carefully displaying them in an orderly fashion on the mantel. this book is about the utter insufficiency of love languages. this book is about how to handle humiliation in public, & the fact that you will still just need to *keep going*. this book is about how my left hand will never know what my left elbow feels like, & how that means that there will always be some corner of the cosmos that I'll never truly know. this book is about rejecting the monster you made. this book is about concrete ideas & abstract paintings. this book seeks to resolve the question. this book seeks to find the language. this book tries to mouth an answer. this book fights the power. this book kicks ass. this book ricochets. this book mimics lego & forgets about discourse. this book does so at its peril. this book needs two for its tango to go. this book is about all the trash, detritus, waste, junk, rubbish, flotsam, jetsam, non-nutritive food, sewage, effluvium, shit, surplus, dirt, mess, weeds, recycling, scraps, leftovers, unwanted discarded useless nonfunctional dysfunctional abandoned unwelcome rejected rejected thrice-rejected garbage that we've managed to twist the only particles in the universe that we have meaningful access to into. this book is about that book.

THANKS & ACKNOWLEDGEMENTS

Love & language work best when shared, & I've been lucky enough to be surrounded by people who give freely of both.

I've done my best to insert clear dedications & homages to poems & poets in the body of this collection, but I do need to declare the debt to Donato Mancini's project *Ligature* (http://eclipsearchive.org/projects/ligature/) – my poem 'interminglings' is a poor imitation.

Susan Holbrook, for being a mentor, a model, a tater whipper, an earl of ink, & a total riot. (& for the title, & for igniting every poem in this collection with her attention & generous suggestions. You're the best editor I could ask for – thanks thanks thanks!)

Alana Wilcox & the team at Coach House, for the enormous investment of effort, faith, energy, resources, skill, & goodwill that makes any book, including this one, possible.

My colleagues: Michael Parrish Lee, for helping me get this project on the right track. James McGrath, for unfailing support. We're doing this. Julia Banister, for sagacity & discernment at the level of the word, & a key line in 'simple math.' Adele Jackson for her enthusiasm & good vibes.

Derek Beaulieu, for being just plain lovel-y & language-y.

My fellow Ledbury Critics (too numerous to mention), & organizers Sandeep Parmar, Sarah Howe, Alycia Pirmohamed, Vidyan Ravinthiran, & Dave Coates, for being a scintillating example of what a poetic & critical community can be.

Jordan Mitchell, Laila Malik, & Keshia Starrett, for reading & responding to drafts at various points.

My creative writing students at Leeds Beckett University, for inspiring me to think openly about love & language, even when everyday life was anything but lovely or worth language-ing about. Specific thanks to Lizzie Thompson for her insight into 'if I had to say.'

Lisa Robertson & the collected residents at the Banff Centre for the Arts, Winter Residency, January 2023, for being a mountain of language among the mountains. Specific thanks to Julie Mannell for gifting me with a hilarious (but adapted) line in 'say what you will.'

The Kramers, the Kraggs, & the Kramersons, for the ongoing extravaganza.

Finally, & always, to Kaley – there's just not enough language to say it, but there is.

POSTCREDITSPOEM

this is your book.

(i'm just writing it.)

(with thanksandloveandlanguage to you, dear reader.)